Fragile

poems by

Cheryl Hopson

Finishing Line Press
Georgetown, Kentucky

Fragile

Copyright © 2017 by Cheryl Hopson
ISBN 978-1-63534-307-6 First Edition
All rights reserved under International and Pan-American Copyright Conventions. No part of this book may be reproduced in any manner whatsoever without written permission from the publisher, except in the case of brief quotations embodied in critical articles and reviews.

ACKNOWLEDGMENTS

I would like to thank Carmel Mawle for publishing an earlier version of "One Death Becomes Another and Another" and "Sister" in *Writing for Peace: Refugees and the Displaced*; Pat Berryhill for publishing "Lost Siblings," "Let the Haunting Come," and an earlier version of "Skating Demons" in *Wraith Infirmity Muses*; and Whitnee Thorpe for publishing "Constellations" in *Wounwapi / we write*.

Publisher: Leah Maines

Editor: Christen Kincaid

Cover Art and Design: Tad Branham

Author Photo: Cheryl Hopson

Printed in the USA on acid-free paper.
Order online: www.finishinglinepress.com
 also available on amazon.com

Author inquiries and mail orders:
Finishing Line Press
P. O. Box 1626
Georgetown, Kentucky 40324
U. S. A.

Table of Contents

Moderate Emotions 1
Hide Don't Hide 2
For So Many Years I Couldn't See You 3
Alice Says It's All the Same 4
One Death Becomes Another and Another 5
Skirting Demons 6
Let the Haunting Come 7
Lost Siblings 8
Sister 9
September 11, 2001 10
My Sisters' Bones 11
Scaffolding 12
The Trip 13
Constellations 14
I Think of Alice and Otis 15
Ambivalent Love 16
Nature Asserts Itself 17
My Sisters' Bones, Continued 18
This Reckoning 20
Wild Cats 21
Her Woman Self 22
'She's gone' 23
Four poems 24
I Collect Your Poems 25
Life calls 26
Melos 27
Dear Audre 28

To Michelle

Moderate moder ate your emotions

A downward spin a twirl up one minute down
all the way down for a day or so after
Word

3am showers regular as sunrise

Old habits breathe their last breath you
Think
A new feeling emerges   I cannot go outside
There is nothing to protect me
This feeling of fragility this this sense my
Sense of my own mortality so fucking real
For the first time. For years I did not
Go
I did not go outside and
Who could know
Would know? I went to work and
Did my job.

But on the inside where the living took place,
I died.

Hide don't hide
Be yourself don't be yourself don't be

Read a word each day to obliterate the emotion
Crawl inside
Go deeper

Days will show their beauty everything
A surprise

The nights will be different
The nights will take all that you have to keep you
Alive

Night, streetlights and the straining
Of Whitney's last album

Som-
Someday some of this will make sense

For so many years I couldn't see you
One life eclipsed by another, I
Did not even think of you
Until recently

Now I see the sunlight sometimes
The sunlight and the shade
Of trees
The leaves orange and red and yellow
Some days, a bouquet of green

I can hear the chatter of neighbors on their balcony
The old white woman with her teased white hair
And rouge

The door returns
Then the stairs, then
My uncle's painting on the wall

But what is this remembering and
Why? Now now I remember now now now
I remember I remember I remember

Me.

Alice says it's all the same
Story
That pulls you in slow   Like
A woman sure of herself like
A lover

Missed
I have been looking for you
Have done this before and before.

You know the story the old
Weathered script today was
Rough

Staticky but I am, for the most part,
Centered. You have many
Brothers and sisters, children of my intellect
But the feeling is strong

Are you so arrogant as to judge your ancestors
Fiery, fiery speaker who calls me to your alter, the one
we share. I drop to my knees, you
Bless me, this time, this time
You forgive me
Forgive me: I gave up drinking
I gave up pleasing others
I chose to take the long view, past
the chaos of brush, beyond
the kindling of old dried woodenness.
No life in me I gave
That up

One death becomes another and another I go to take cover the blinding light
Is the last thing I see

I'm bleeding out leaving my body
My body
Becomes a shell emptied of its wealth

I crawl along the floor of the damned seeking
Refuge from this, our shared life or
What is it? This is hell

The wind picks up. And winter becomes spring becomes fall becomes
Itself again a decade
disappears, fades
My mouth takes on a permanent frown.

This is lo-
Loss or love?

Wait. Wait. Don't go. The voice cries out
You don't stop, don't listen.

See the bees buzzing and feel that fear

Drill a hole into your spine a hole
into your heart
Become unable to see, become
unable

This is the violence of creation

Skirting Demons

Aretha sings,

"I know everything is
gonna be alright," and I play
call-and-response,
skirting demons until the gate of memory
swings wide open, and a dark-eyed
black girl
in a bright yellow shirt, smiles,
waving into the future.

Let the haunting come
night after night
Let the dream do its work,
Be a canvas: A steel-white glider,
and air thick with the scent of honeysuckle
and roses.

You and she talk and glide, and
I am satisfied to be in your company.

I am a bridge
between, a variation on theme

Lady Lazarus with a made-up face in
varying shades of brown.

I speak and tell a story of lo-
sing.

Lost Siblings

I imagine our difference as a flower garden
some of us are tulips,
sturdy-stemmed and bulbous
some of us are azaleas, overgrown and wild /
tiger lilies, cottonweed and bougainvillea.
Some of us do not yet have a name.
We are a tribe of lost siblings, with
the shocked look of the left behind.

There is loss at our center and
the people we were are no more.

Sister,

For five years,
I've cried
and wondered and
forgotten and remembered
and still
I listen for your footsteps and
in dreams dial numbers that reach
no one.
My eyes become telescopic
in their search for you.
But there is nothing, save an outline—no flesh with
extra-ness and color; no voice calling out in
adoration or hesitation,
"sister".
I look for you in symbols, and
seek comfort in the eavesdropping of
memory.

September 11, 2001

The people hold
hands and leap as
the fireball blazes.
I go to shield my eyes until
a voice from the inside says,
look: at this, their refusal to die
alone and by fire.
This leap is not flight. It is
audacious.

My Sisters' Bones

how can bones be of use?
bones do not speak back,
bones do not get up and walk
away when they tire of listening.
and what are bones without flesh
to juice the marrow?
i want to look into the eyes of women for whom I am
a palimpsest
i want to push back cuticles on the nails of hands I admire
i want to forget about bones.
but, my sisters'
bones compel me to them; to
battle the dirt that holds them, to beat at it
with the arrogance and fists of a younger sister; to
kick and scream and howl my way back to
them to
me to
life.

Scaffolding

Some poems write themselves;
The line listens and breaks, knowing its place.
Other poems have to be built, metaphor by
metaphor—you've heard this before.
Some poems are scaffolding, a holding in place while
the muse goes in search of form.
Writing this, I think of Antoni
Gaudi sleeping inside the womb of his creation.
Weeks turn into months, for him,
turn into years, for us, and
a cathedral begins its reaching, and
takes shape.
He must have known that creativity is inviolate;
that structure can be a reprieve
I think of the train he did not see
or was unseen by, and long to look upon his creation.
Night comes, and a poem finds its subject.

The Trip

a recurring childhood drama
you became the changeling
bullying step—

and I became silence,
the always disappointed,
angry, fearing girl
child, learned in

the discordant
rhythms of intimate relations—

I knew you long before
we met.

Constellations

1. a rainbow forms on asphalt
2. stalactites drip baptismal-like on foreheads
a poem comes
3. the sun blazes, then sets and turns a blue sky to lavender
a poem hums a tune in my ear
4. constellations force the head up and I seek out
the North Star—a habit.
a poem announces its title—
5. eyes instigate lines: "This is how you move /
as close as one can / ... / to me."

I think of Alice and Otis,

both going as far West as possible
without leaving the continental United
States; both leaving
to breathe.

Alice saying,
I have the whole of the Rocky
Mountain Range between
Me and thee,
Georgia.

Otis writing a song about it.

Which tells me: when you want to give
in, don't.

When fear becomes bile in your mouth,
swallow hard.

There is no guarantee of strength tomorrow.
Keep
stepping.

Ambivalent Love

The storm comes, and I run from
Air thick with reverberations of "I'm
sorry." Ambivalent love
is wasteful, and an oxymoron. Sethe said
it best: all, or nothing.

I notice more the paltriness of our
pretty words and smiles; the resonances
of a childhood among thieves.

I admit to not seeing. I did not know
that grief could carry over and lay claim. But
being is its own difficulty. Why complicate it
with blame?

No more apologizing.

Nature Asserts Itself

You can't assert dominance over
what is natural, a
tree, for example, unless
you chop it down and
make sure to remove its roots.
Birds will chirp
in spite of your sour mood, your
disinterest in bird song; a baby gets born
cries, and takes its place, and
flowers will bloom

We have only so long
to fight
and make love; to
laugh and create a mess.
Let's lock eyes
and get to know each other and,
while we're at it, let's dance.

My Sisters' Bones, Continued

*And I am to put flowers
On their graves—T loved sunflowers,
But for M, I'm not sure.*

I have visited with them many times in the space between sleep and wake.
We have spent much time together, there.

Blood of my blood.

My sisters' bones

are of no use to me.

Bones do not speak back or get up and walk away
When they tire of listening.

But I know I need them, to return
to them, to see with my own eyes
names etched on stones,
plastic or real flowers Mama leaves for
mother's day and Christmas

Is it too much to hope for
blue skies
and a welcoming seat?

I will not ask again *why*
they left, but I will battle
Myself and the dirt that holds them

I imagine their spirits looking up or
down and saying, "Even in death,
a nuisance."

And I will press my ear to the cold
hard earth and listen for the silence I expect as
bones do not speak.
Bones are not flesh.

My mind knows this.
My heart knows different.

This Reckoning

I never learned
to sew or knit
or quilt   But I sprinkle the land
With words, as my oldest sister instructed—
"Write our story," the last words
Said to me before the call,
The falling down
The falling

This is the treasure—to try my hand at
something we both loved, to leave behind this
reckoning, this beautiful,
daily reckoning.

Wild Cats

I remember being startled by your tattoo of a black panther,

in repose across the canvas of your chest
its red streaks suggesting torn flesh—

All our life together, I was frightened
By your refusal to be good.

Now that you're gone, I am startled by
my blind willingness

Sister, I want to set the world on fire
to eradicate my need of respect-
ability

In sleep I dream of a white lion
in my path—see the wild in its eyes,
the mangy coat,

the arrogance of the leash—

I know the white lion is me, Sister,
worn-out, But wild, still

and daring.

Her Woman Self

A woman I love sits at a Formica table,
In 1983, and takes a drag off a Virginia Slims

Light

White coffee cools in a Styrofoam
cup—

as her husband speaks

his voice is gruff; he walks
heavy-footed
it sounds like anger, like

arrogance

Three decades later I push
myself to go back, to the woman,

with her shaded gray eyes

My grandmother,
her woman self

then, as now.

'She's gone'

I close my eyes and run
my fingers over the page

trying to see
trying to drown out my unspoken
words, my thoughts

My mind goes and goes

I pull back the curtain of memory, after
all these years, go back to the day before
you died

and
remember
How good it felt
to be alive

before your daughter's voice,
like polished stones,
called to say, "She's gone."

Four poems

Built from fragments,
Simmering on the back burner of
my mind

This is the only way I know to put
worry in its place

Filling pages

I build this thing, Sister, this thing that
Says we had each other

I do all I can do,
then close the book, and let music
do the rest

I collect your poems on the old floppy
disk of memory

and put Shakespeare to the test—
"so long as men can breathe"

I revive you.

Life calls
and for two decades I answer—

I put myself on overseas flights,
escape to books, and new places, and new
faces become my normal, and missing

becomes my every day.

"All story begins with melody." ~Sonny Rollins

Melos

swing down, sweet melos,

like a jesus-devoted distraction
and i will follow,

disciple to your melody

will bear the sting of ridicule
breaking bread with
madonned whores, go the way of crucifixes,
if only you'll

rock me.

i will
conjure word,

incantation to a god offered in jest;

will push white-sheeted sound out

till its lush and right, galvanize scat
in minor musings seeped to marrow

if only you'll
rock me.

swing on down, sweet melos,

all story begins
with you,

black notes pitching "savior, will you

rock me,
rock me,
rock me
easy?"

Dear Audre,

A student comes to me and says,
"But I love her, and I want others to love her,
So what should I do?"

And this is when I remember mangoes,
Oatmeal cookies, and impatience, three vices
You laid claim to—

Of mangoes—I like the green-orange, yellow-
red tautness of its skin, the
soft insularity of its fruit, the tease on the tongue
a reminder of
a woman that I love.

Of oatmeal cookies—greedily, I want them
as years ago I wanted you, no matter that we'd never meet,
no matter that
my body can not process
the sweet.

Of impatience—a feeling
I've come to recognize as love.

Cheryl Hopson has a PhD in English from the University of Kentucky. She is an assistant professor of African American Studies in the Department of Diversity and Community Studies at Western Kentucky University in Bowling Green, Kentucky. Cheryl is originally from Southwest Virginia, and is an essayist and poet.

www.ingramcontent.com/pod-product-compliance
Lightning Source LLC
LaVergne TN
LVHW041511070426
835507LV00012B/1497